Lines crisscross deserts and oceans,
flow along rivers and mountains.

Birds and fish can cross them freely,
but boats and airplanes cannot.

BORDERS

Written by Gudol
Illustrated by Haerang

Translated by Sophie Bowman

If you open a map of the world, you will see a patchwork of countries pieced together like a jigsaw puzzle. This is because over 200 countries divide up the land on Earth without leaving any gaps. Examine the map closely, and you will notice that some lines are curvy and some are straight. These lines, which divide countries and draw their boundaries, are called borders. Have you ever tried crossing one?

CANADA

To cross a border into another country, you must first receive permission. You have to prove who you are by showing a passport, and you may need a visa to confirm you are allowed in. If an illness is going around, you may have to be screened, and people with symptoms might be quarantined until the sickness has passed.

Then there is customs, where luggage is checked for anything that is not permitted. Plants, fruits, or seeds could carry harmful pests, so they cannot cross into another country. Pets can only cross borders after going through a strict screening process.

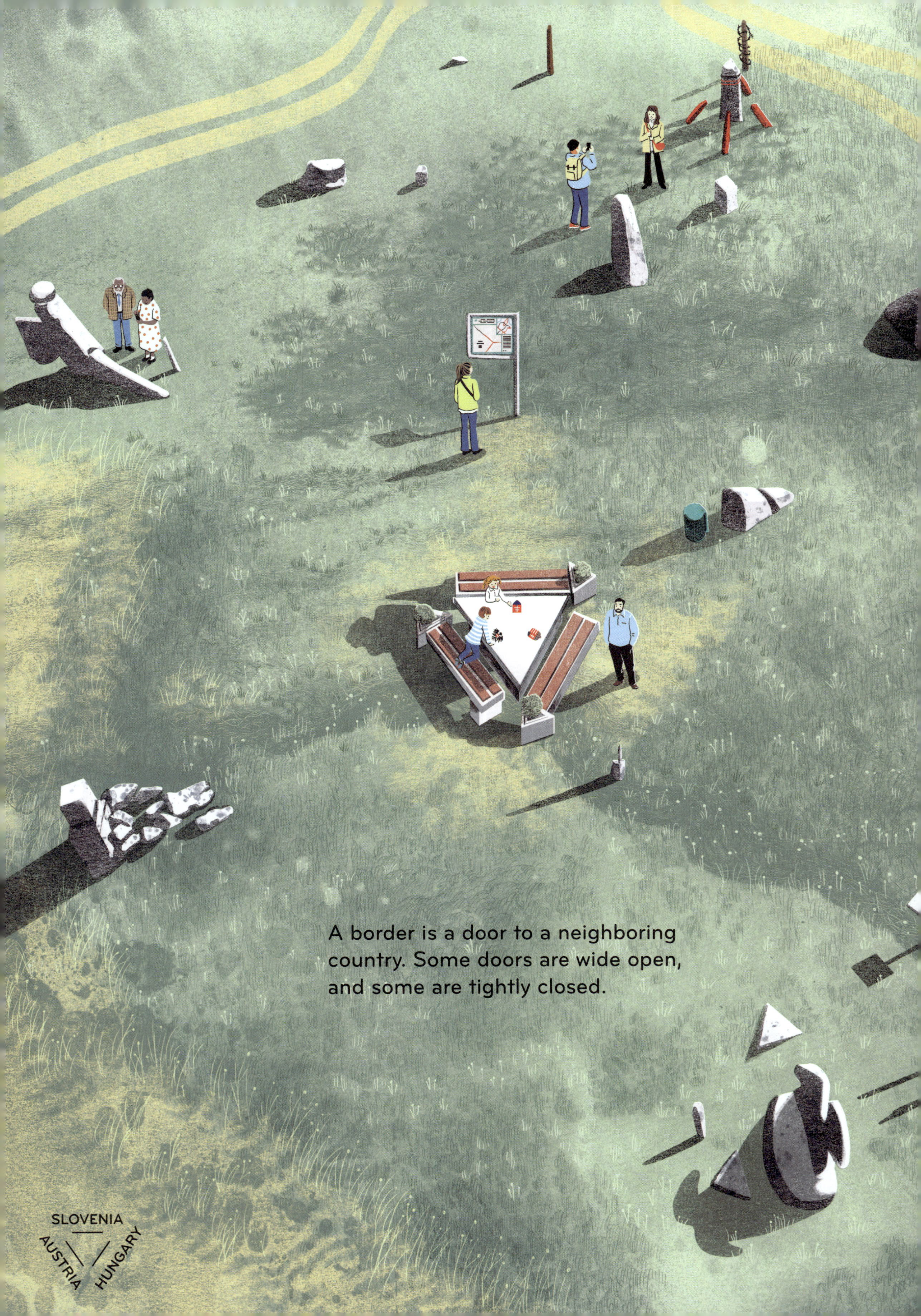

A border is a door to a neighboring country. Some doors are wide open, and some are tightly closed.

Sometimes doors that are open can suddenly shut, and doors that are shut can suddenly open, too.

A border is a place where different worlds meet.
When you cross a border, languages and letters can change,

SOUTH KOREA | CHINA

and the money people use can change, too.

TURKMENISTAN | IRAN

What people eat can change,

GREECE | TURKEY

and how they look and dress can also be very different.

EGYPT | SUDAN

The date can change,

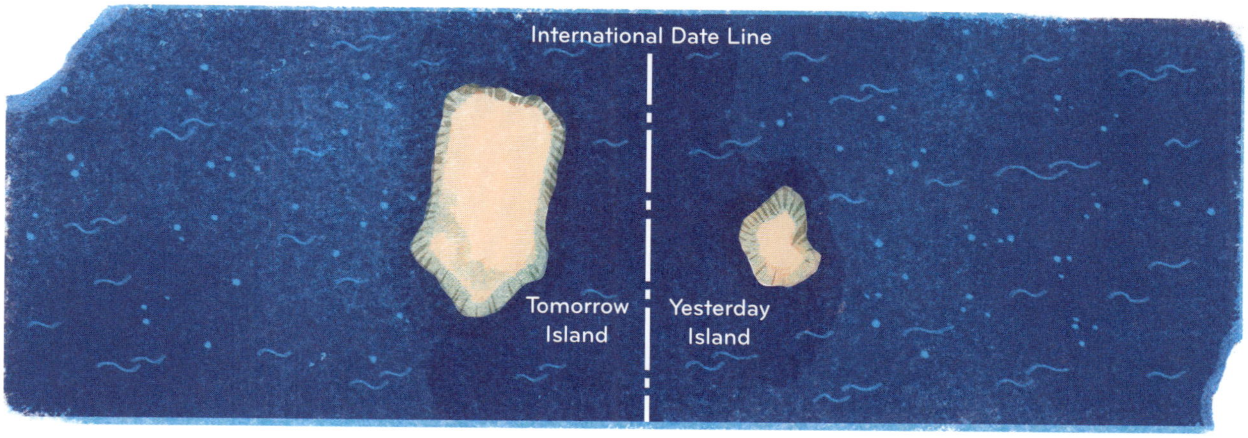

RUSSIA | U.S.A.

and people might practice different religions,

INDIA | PAKISTAN

use different gestures to say the same thing,

CHINA | KOREA | JAPAN

or drive on the opposite side of the road.

VENEZUELA | GUYANA

Borders can tell us a lot about the relationship between neighboring countries. The borders of the same country can look completely different, depending on which country is on the other side. Just like this country you see here.

CANADA | U.S.A.

U.S.A. | MEXICO

At borders, people from neighboring countries meet. There are places where communities gather to hold markets to buy and sell goods.

Across Asia, Europe, Africa, and South America, there are all kinds of border markets open for trade.

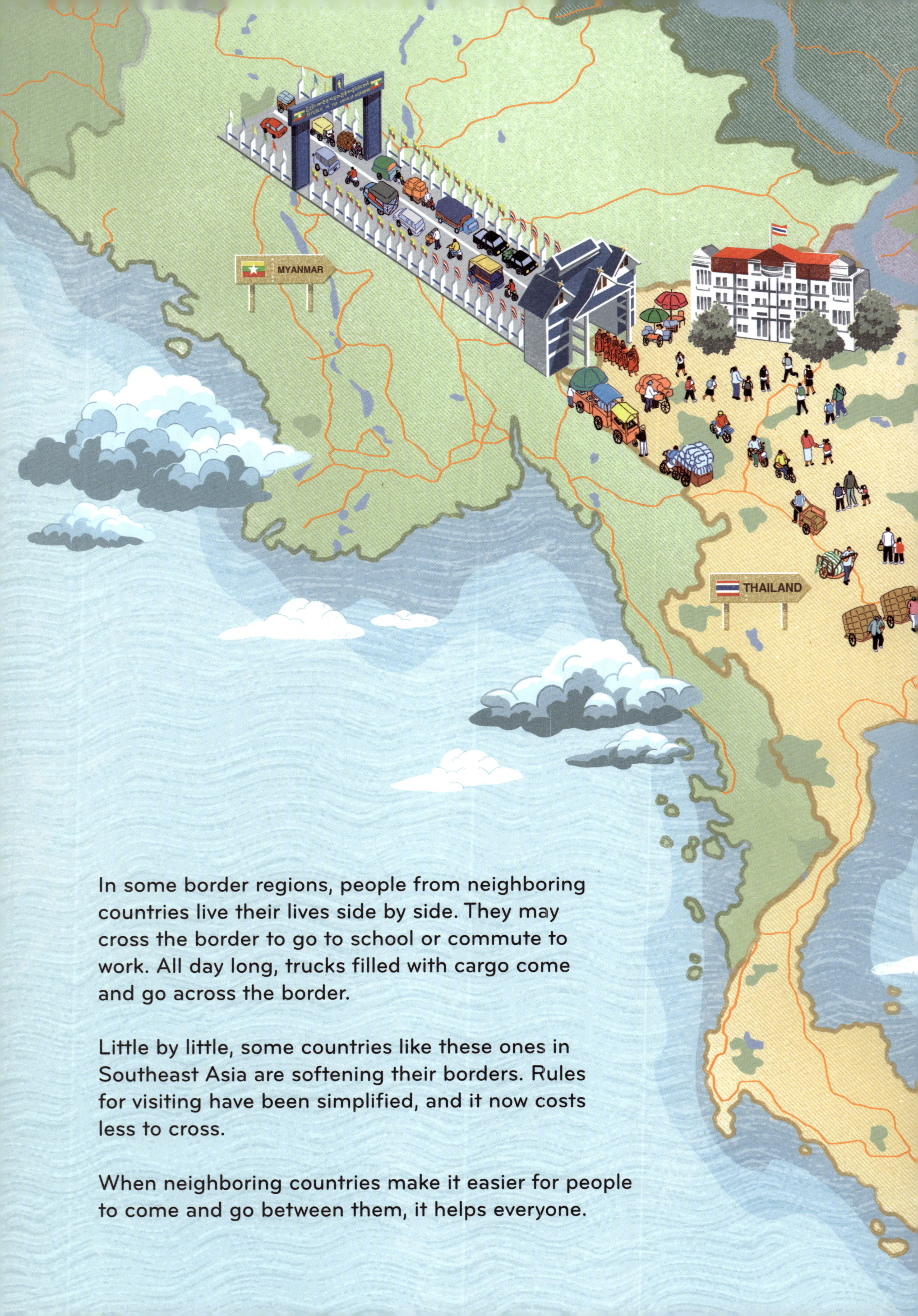

In some border regions, people from neighboring countries live their lives side by side. They may cross the border to go to school or commute to work. All day long, trucks filled with cargo come and go across the border.

Little by little, some countries like these ones in Southeast Asia are softening their borders. Rules for visiting have been simplified, and it now costs less to cross.

When neighboring countries make it easier for people to come and go between them, it helps everyone.

LAOS
VIETNAM
CAMBODIA

There is even a region where many countries live as one, without borders. It's called the European Union. For more than twenty years, people and goods have moved freely within this region. It began with just six countries opening their doors to one another, and slowly many more joined, although one chose to close its doors again recently.

In the European Union, citizens can live or work wherever they like, and more than twenty of its countries share a central bank and use the same currency.

Here there are no checkpoints, no walls between countries. Borders are marked only with flags and signs, or lines painted on roads, or stone monuments, or even just a stick.

There is even a border that cuts a town into dozens of pieces—it crosses through buildings and roads, passing under doors and dining tables. People in this town cross the border between the two countries dozens of times each day.

BELGIUM | NETHERLANDS

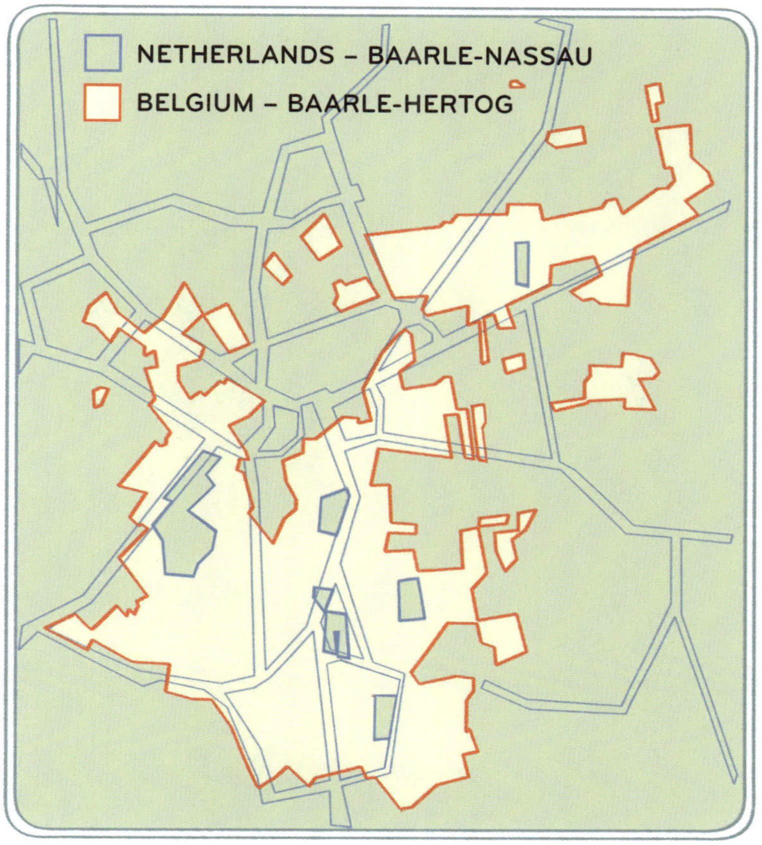

In this town, called Baarle, there are two mayors, two town halls, and two post offices. The town has two official names, two town signs, and two churches. Here the citizens of two countries live together in one town and get along peacefully.

But not all borders are places where you can easily meet neighbors. Some borders cross the Sahara, the world's largest desert, and others follow the ridges of the highest mountain range in the world, the Himalayas.

CHINA | NEPAL

Sometimes countries are separated by nature: split apart by a long river, a massive waterfall, a thick forest, or a vast sea.

But people build roads—up and down mountains that pierce the clouds, through deserts that sizzle in the sun, above canyons and roaring waterfalls that shake the earth and sky, and across lands cradled by the sea. From the distant past to the present day, people have made roads to bridge the space between borders.

SWEDEN
DENMARK

People have crossed borders for as long as borders have existed.

Merchants crossed them with precious wares to sell,

people of faith crossed them to spread their religion,

and explorers crossed borders, curious to see other places.

Greedy invaders crossed borders,

and so did independence fighters to liberate their colonized lands,

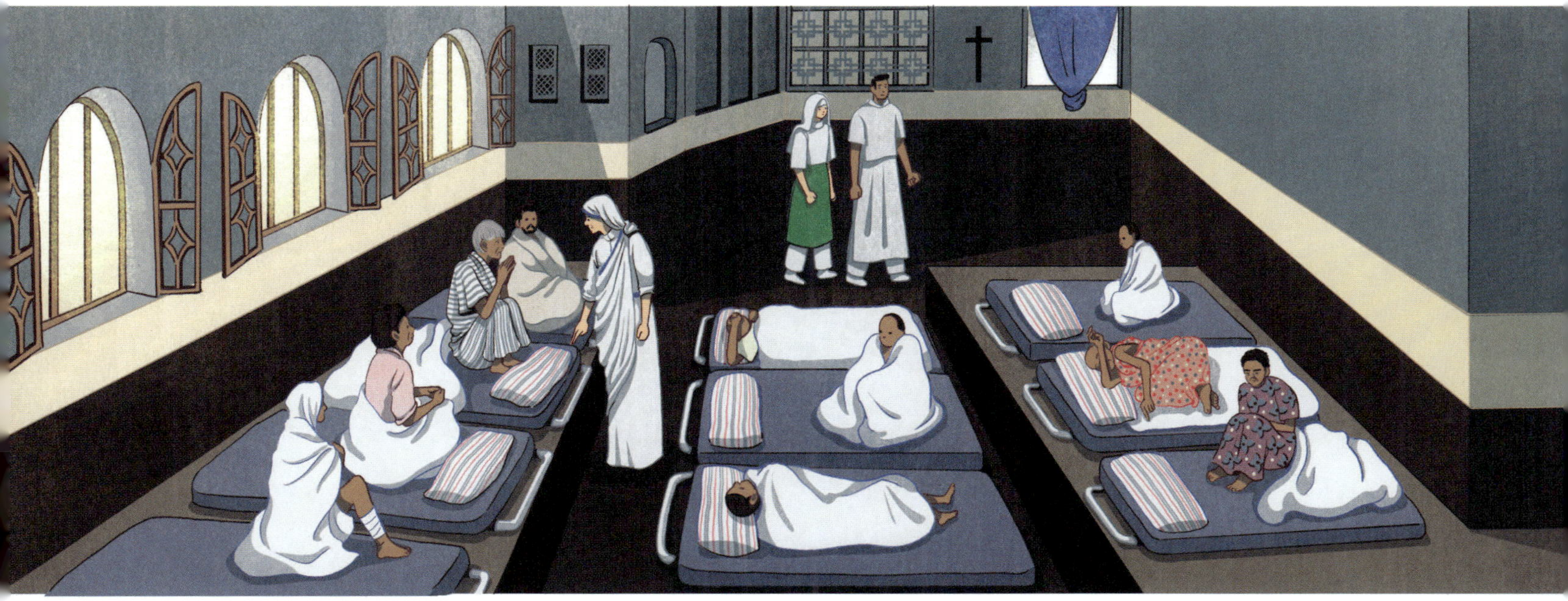

and nurses and doctors to care for the sick or wounded.

Right now, too, there are people crossing borders. Students cross borders to study, and workers cross borders in search of jobs. Travelers cross borders to discover new cultures, and refugees who cannot stay in their homelands cross borders because they have no other choice.

But sometimes, at borders, there are walls...

To try to keep out people of a different religion

or those of a different ethnicity,

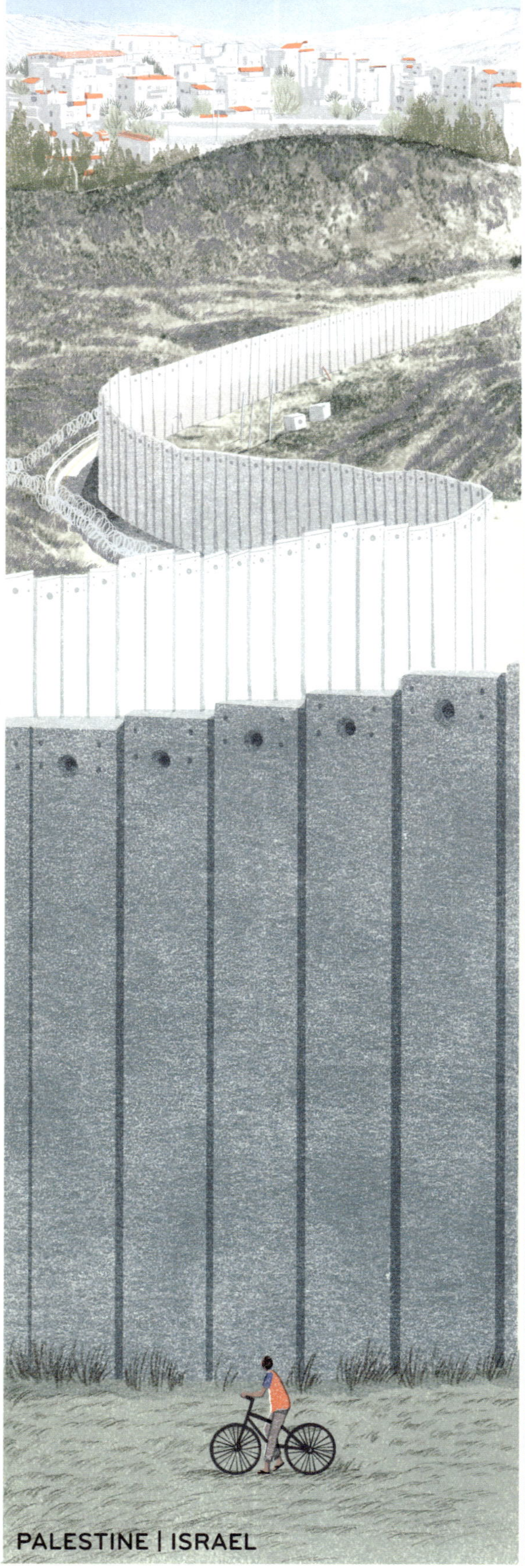

to end conflicts over resources,

for fear of terrorism,

to exclude refugees,

or to stop a disease from spreading.

People have constructed long, tall barriers at borders. Today, there are more than seventy border walls separating countries around the world.

GERMAN DEMOCRATIC REPUBLIC (EAST GERMANY)

FEDERAL REPUBLIC OF GERMANY (WEST GERMANY)

There was also once a wall that divided one country into two.

A wall that separated people who spoke the same language and shared the same culture.

The people of Germany tore that wall down.

It took forty years for the two parts to become one country again.

But other countries have not been able to become one again, even after seventy years. Enough time has passed for a young child to become a grandparent, but the families separated by the wall still long to see each other.

DEMOCRATIC PEOPLE'S REPUBLIC OF KOREA (NORTH KOREA)

REPUBLIC OF KOREA (SOUTH KOREA)

AH1
KAESONG INDUSTRIAL COMPLEX
Sinuiju
Hamhung
GYEONGUI LINE
PYONGYANG
GYEONGWON LINE
Sariwon
Kaesong
Munsan
SEOUL
Daejeon
INTER-KOREAN TRANSIT OFFICE
SINUIJU - BUSAN
SEOUL INTERNATIONAL STATION
SEOUL INTERNATIONAL STATION
SEOUL - PARIS

In the spring of 2018, the leaders of these two countries held hands and crossed the border together. It was a small step but a big promise for unity on the Korean Peninsula. When the two are reunited as one, there will finally be peace on this land.

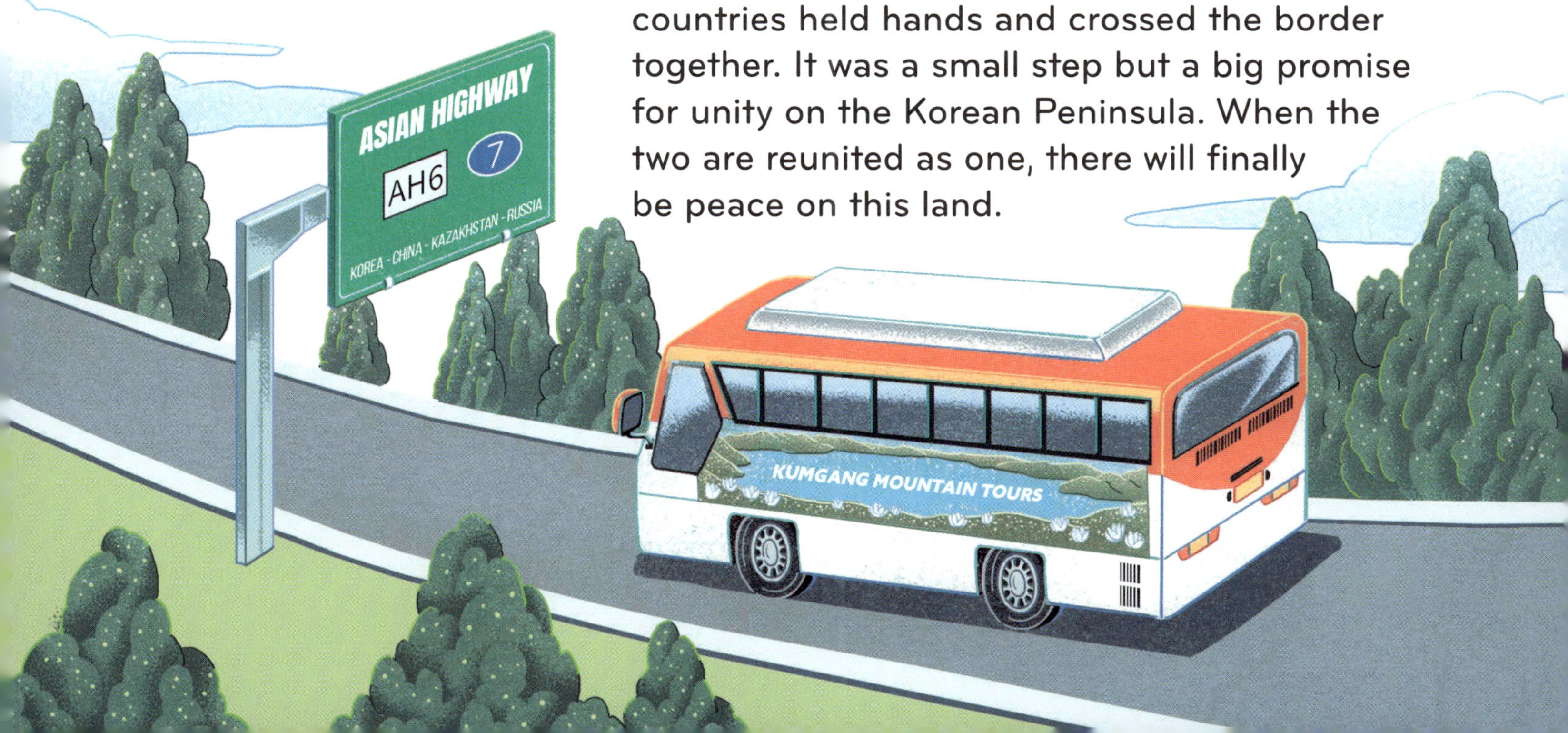

In other places, borders suddenly appear or disappear. Since 2002, at least five countries, including East Timor, have gained independence from other countries. When this happens, new border lines are drawn on world maps.

Palestine Great March of Return

There is also a country whose borders have been erased from maps, as if to say that it is no longer a nation. But, to this day, the people there refuse to be forgotten and strive to reclaim what was taken from them.

Conflicts can easily spark at borders. This is because they are more than just lines drawn on the ground. Although we cannot always see them, borders stretch out across sky and land, and into the sea.

Earth and its oceans hold valuable resources like oil, gas, minerals, and fish. Many countries strive to protect their resources, or want to claim more for themselves. If neighboring countries disagree about their borders, they can struggle to get along.

ARGENTINA | CHILE

But people around the world have made all kinds of efforts to bring peace to borders. At one border where there was a long conflict over territory, a statue of Jesus was raised.

On another continent, citizens of two countries once divided by religion now meet at the border each day for a flag-lowering ceremony.

Artists cover border walls with artwork,

ISRAEL
PALESTINE

and religious leaders go to border walls to hold special services.

But no matter how high a border stands, there are things that walls cannot stop. While boats and planes may not cross borders without permission, the birds and fish that migrate with the seasons know no borders.

Air and water, the most important resources for human life, cross borders freely, too. When smog drifts over from neighboring countries, people cannot play outside or open their windows, and the pollution from factories in one country creates acid rain that falls on its neighbors.

After a nuclear accident in another country, fish polluted with radiation can reach our dinner tables. And greenhouse gases melt ice caps, raising water levels and flooding islands in the Pacific Ocean.

We are all connected, even across borders. Roads and railways, flight paths and sea routes, and oil and gas pipelines link countries and cities.

Radio waves and the internet also connect everyone on Earth. We can find out what's happening in another country in real time, and can have face-to-face conversations with people on the other side of the world.

We enjoy foods that have crossed borders, and we use many things that have crossed borders. We read books and listen to songs that come to us from across borders. Look around you. So much of what we cherish comes from other countries.

Religion, philosophy, the arts, culture, science, and technology have also traveled back and forth across borders throughout history, enriching our lives and shaping the world we live in today.

A world where more than 200 countries live together as neighbors. A place we call planet Earth.

ABOUT THE AUTHOR

Gudol studied photography at university, and after graduation, she spent 28 months backpacking around the world. Following her travels, she lived in India before returning to Korea. She is the author of *Borders* (2021) and *Seven Grandmas and the Playground* (2022). She also self-published *How to Cross Barriers*, and the art book *1-4-All: All 14 Consonants of the Korean Alphabet (2024)*. She was awarded the Prix Sorcières (2025), the Korea Publication Culture Prize (2022), the Golden Goblin Award (2022), the Taiwan Open Book Award (2023), and the Korea Andersen Award in the children's poetry category (2015). Gudol currently lives and works in Seoul, Korea.

Instagram: @gudolrion

ABOUT THE ILLUSTRATOR

Haerang is an illustrator who explores the invisible threads woven by the beings dwelling throughout daily life. She translates the subtle, unfamiliar sensations captured in nature and travel into visual narratives. Her work includes illustrations for various books, such as *Borders*, as well as covers for numerous literary works. Additionally, she has self-published image-centric books, including *Aurora Travelogue* and *Tenggeri – 27 Days in Mongolia*.

Instagram: @space_radiation

Scan the QR code to download the Educator's Guide for this book.

Or go to: helvetiq.com/us/borders-us

Helvetiq is being supported by the Swiss Federal Office of Culture
with a structural grant for the years 2026–2028.

BORDERS
Meeting Our Neighbors Around the World

Originally published as:
국경 (Borders)

First published in Korean by Bear Books Inc.
Translation from Korean: Sophie Bowman

ISBN: 978-3-03964-149-9
First edition in English: 2026
Printed in Czech Republic

Av. de l'Église-Anglaise 2
CH-1006 Lausanne
Switzerland

HEL·· VETIQ helvetiq.com

FSC www.fsc.org MIX Paper from responsible sources FSC® C014138